FIRST GRACES

Illustrated by
TASHA TUDOR

Lutterworth Press

First published in Great Britain, 1964

This impression 1985

Lutterworth Press
7 All Saints' Passage
Cambridge CB2 3LS
England

ISBN 0 7188 0307 8

Printed in Singapore

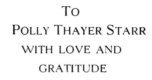

To
POLLY THAYER STARR
WITH LOVE AND
GRATITUDE

Dear Lord, I offer Thee this day
All I shall think, or do, or say.

For food, and all Thy gifts of love,
    We give Thee thanks and praise.
Look down, O Father, from above
    And bless us all our days.

For what we are about to receive,
the Lord make us truly thankful.

Some hae meat, and canna eat,
    And some wad eat that want it;
But we hae meat and we can eat,
    And sae the Lord be thankit.
Robert Burns

For every cup and plateful,
God make us truly grateful.

A. S. T. Fisher

Bless, O Lord, this food to our use,

And us to Thy loving service.

God, we thank You for this food,
For rest and home and all things good;
For wind and rain and sun above,
But most of all for those we love.

Maryleona Frost

Be present at our table, Lord;
Be here and everywhere adored.
Thy creatures bless, and grant that we
May feast in paradise with Thee.

John Wesley

We thank Thee, Lord, for happy hearts,
For rain and sunny weather.
We thank Thee, Lord, for this our food,
And that we are together.

Emilie Fendall Johnson

Jesus, friend of little children,
Be a friend to me;
Take my hand and ever keep me
Close to Thee.

Walter J. Mathans

T. Tudor
1955

23

The Lord my pasture shall prepare,
And feed me with a shepherd's care;
His presence shall my wants supply,
And guard me with a watchful eye.

Joseph Addison

At the New Year

Thanks be to Thee, Lord Jesus,
For another year to serve Thee,
To love Thee,
And to praise Thee.

A BIRTHDAY GRACE

God made the sun
  And God made the tree,
God made the mountains
  And God made me.

I thank You, O God,
   For the sun and the tree,
For making the mountains
   And for making me.

Leah Gale

29

At Easter

Joyfully, this Easter day,
I kneel, a little child, to pray;
Jesus, who hath conquered death,
Teach me, with my every breath,
To praise and worship Thee.

Sharon Banigan

SPRINGTIME

All things bright and beautiful,
All creatures great and small,
All things wise and wonderful,
The Lord God made them all.

Each little flower that opens,
Each little bird that sings,
He made their glowing colours,
He made their tiny wings.

Mrs. C. F. Alexander

FOR SCHOOL

At home or at school
Wherever I may go
One thought I remember
That is good to know.
It stays in my heart
A happy little song
That God takes care of me
The whole day long.

J. Lilian Vandevere

34

For the beauty of the earth,
For the beauty of the skies,
For the love which from our birth
Over and around us lies,

For the beauty of each hour,
Of the day and of the night,
Hill and vale, and tree and flower,
Sun and moon, and stars of light,

Gracious God, to Thee we raise
This our sacrifice of praise.

F. S. Pierpoint

Thank You for the world so sweet,
Thank You for the food we eat,
Thank You for the birds that sing,
Thank You, God, for everything.

E. Rutter Leatham

38

THANKSGIVING

May God give us grateful hearts
And keep us mindful
Of the need of others.

CHRISTMAS EVE

What can I give Him,
   Poor as I am?
   If I were a shepherd,
I would bring a lamb;
   If I were a wise man,
   I would do my part:
But what I can I give Him!
   Give my heart.

Christina Rossetti

CHRISTMAS DAY

Glory to God in the highest,
and on earth peace,
good will toward men.

Luke 2:14

44

WE OFFER sincere thanks to the various publishers and copyright holders for permission to reprint; "Dear Lord, I offer thee this day" from *Prayers for All Occasions*, Forward Movement Publications of the Episcopal Church; "For food, and all thy gifts of love" from *A Little Book of Prayers and Graces*, by Quail Hawkins, illustrated by Marguerite de Angeli; copyright 1941, 1952 by Doubleday & Co., Inc.; "For every cup and plateful" from *An Anthology of Prayers*, by A. S. T. Fisher, copyright 1934 by Longmans, Green & Co.; "God, we thank you for this food," by Maryleona Frost, *Wee Wisdom*; "We thank thee, Lord, for happy hearts" from *A Little Book of Prayers*, by Emilie Fendall

thai
david smyth

For over 60 years, more than 40 million people have learnt over 750 subjects the **teach yourself** way, with impressive results.

be where you want to be
with **teach yourself**

For UK order enquiries: please contact Bookpoint Ltd., 130 Milton Park, Abingdon, Oxon OX14 4SB. Telephone: +44 (0) 1235 827720. Fax: +44 (0) 1235 400454. Lines are open 09.00–18.00, Monday to Saturday, with a 24-hour message answering service. You can also order through our website www.madaboutbooks.com.

For USA order enquiries: please contact McGraw-Hill Customer Services, PO Box 545, Blacklick, OH 43004-0545, USA. Telephone: 1-800-722-4726. Fax: 1-614-755-5645.

For Canada order enquiries: please contact McGraw-Hill Ryerson Ltd., 300 Water St, Whitby, Ontario L1N 9B6, Canada. Telephone: 905 430 5000. Fax: 905 430 5020.

Long renowned as the authoritative source for self-guided learning – with more than 30 million copies sold worldwide – the *Teach Yourself* series includes over 300 titles in the fields of languages, crafts, hobbies, business, computing and education.

British Library Cataloguing in Publication Data: a catalogue record for this title is available from The British Library

Library of Congress Catalog Card Number: On file

First published in UK 1995 by Hodder Headline Ltd., 338 Euston Road, London, NW1 3BH.

First published in US 1996 by Contemporary Books, a Division of The McGraw-Hill Companies, 1 Prudential Plaza, 130 East Randolph Street, Chicago, IL 60601 USA.

This edition published 2003.

The 'Teach Yourself' name is a registered trade mark of Hodder & Stoughton Ltd.

Typeset by Graphicraft Limited, Hong Kong

Printed in Great Britain for Hodder & Stoughton Educational, a division of Hodder Headline Ltd., 338 Euston Road, London NW1 3BH by Cox & Wyman Ltd., Reading, Berkshire.

Impression number   10   9   8   7   6   5   4   3   2   1

Year   2007 2006 2005 2004 2003